About the Author

JOE SIMPSON is the author of several bestselling books, of which the first, *Touching the Void,* won both the NCR Award and the Boardman Tasker Award. His later books are *This Game of Ghosts, Storms of Silence, Dark Shadows Falling, The Beckoning Silence* and a novel, *The Water People.*

Joe Simpson

TOUCHING THE VOID

With a Foreword by Chris Bonington

HERMES WI4TH LITTLE FREE LIBRARY

Perennial
An Imprint of HarperCollins*Publishers*

First hardcover edition published in Great Britain in 1988 by Jonathan Cape. First paperback edition published in Great Britain in 2004 by Vintage.

First Perennial edition published 2004.

Library of Congress Cataloging-in-Publication Data
   Simpson, Joe.
      Touching the void / Joe Simpson ; with a foreword by
      Chris Bonington—1st Perennial ed.
         p. cm.
      Originally published: London : J. Cape, 1988.
      ISBN 0-06-073055-2
      1. Simpson, Joe. 2. Mountaineers—Great Britain—
      Biography. 3. Yates, Simon. 4. Mountaineering—
      Peru—Huayhuash, Cordillera. 5. Mountaineering—
      Search and rescue operations—Peru—Huayhuash,
      Cordillera—Case studies. I. Title.
      GV199.92.S57A3 2004
      796.5'22'092—dc22
      [B]   2004042419

04 05 06 07 08 RRD 20 19 18 17 16 15 14 13 12 11

To
SIMON YATES
for a debt I can never repay

And to those friends who have gone to the mountains
and have not returned

CONTENTS

FOREWORD
by Chris Bonington

I first met Joe in Chamonix last winter. Like many climbers he had decided it was time to learn to ski, had no intention of taking formal lessons and was teaching himself. I had heard and read stories about him, of desperately narrow escapes on the mountains, particularly his latest escapade in Peru, but they had made only a limited impact.

Sitting beside him in a bar in Chamonix it was difficult putting the stories and reputation to the person. He was dark, with a slightly punk hairstyle, and there was something abrasive in his manner. I found it difficult to take him in my mind from the streets of Sheffield into the mountains. And I didn't think much more about him until I read the manuscript of *Touching the Void*. It wasn't just the remarkable nature of the story – and it was remarkable, one of the most incredible stories of survival that I have ever read – it was the quality of the writing that was both sensitive and dramatic, capturing the extremes of fear, suffering and emotion both of himself and his partner, Simon Yates. From the moment Joe slipped and fell, breaking his leg on the descent, through his solitary agony in the crevasse until the moment he crawled into their base camp, I was riveted, unable to put the book down.

To put Joe's struggle for survival in perspective, I can compare it to my own experience on the Ogre in 1977, when Doug Scott slipped whilst abseiling from the summit and broke both legs. At this stage the situation was similar to the early part of Joe's ordeal. There were just two of us near the top of a particularly inhospitable mountain. But for us there were two other team members in a snow cave on the col just below the summit block. We were caught by a storm and took six days, five of them without food, to get down. On the way I slipped and broke my ribs. It was the worst experience I have ever had in the mountains and yet, compared to what Joe Simpson went through on his own, it begins to pale.

A close parallel happened on Haramosh in the Karakoram in 1957. It was an Oxford University party trying to make the first ascent of this 24,270 foot peak. They had just decided to turn back; two of the members, Bernard Jillot and John Emery, wanted to go just a little farther on the ridge to get photographs and were swept away in a wind slab avalanche. They survived the fall and their team mates went down to rescue them, but this was only the start of a long-drawn-out catastrophe, from which only two emerged alive.

Theirs, too, was an intriguing and very moving story but it was told by a professional writer and, because of this, lacks the immediacy and strength of someone writing at first hand. This is where Joe Simpson scores. Not only is it one of the most incredible survival stories of which I have heard, it is superbly and poignantly told and deserves to become a classic in this genre.

February 1988

All men dream: but not equally.
Those who dream by night in the dusty
recesses of their minds wake in the day
to find that it was vanity: but the dreamers
of the day are dangerous men, for they may
act their dreams with open eyes, to make it
possible.

T.E. Lawrence, *The Seven Pillars of Wisdom*

KEY
1 1st snow hole
2 2nd snow hole
3 3rd snow hole
4 4th snow hole
A Accident site
X Rope cut
C Cliff and crevasse
a 1st snow hole on crawl
b 2nd night alone
B Bomb alley
---- Ascent & lowers

The crawl-out from the face

I

BENEATH THE MOUNTAIN LAKES

I was lying in my sleeping bag, staring at the light filtering through the red and green fabric of the dome tent. Simon was snoring loudly, occasionally twitching in his dream world. We could have been anywhere. There is a peculiar anonymity about being in tents. Once the zip is closed and the outside world barred from sight, all sense of location disappears. Scotland, the French Alps, the Karakoram, it was always the same. The sounds of rustling, of fabric flapping in the wind, or of rainfall, the feel of hard lumps under the ground sheet, the smell of rancid socks and sweat – these are universals, as comforting as the warmth of the down sleeping bag.

Outside, in a lightening sky, the peaks would be catching the first of the morning sun, with perhaps even a condor cresting the thermals above the tent. That wasn't too fanciful either since I had seen one circling the camp the previous afternoon. We were in the middle of the Cordillera Huayhuash, in the Peruvian Andes, separated from the nearest village by twenty-eight miles of rough walking, and surrounded by the most spectacular ring of ice mountains I had ever seen, and the only indication of this from within our tent was the regular roaring of avalanches falling off Cerro Sarapo.

I felt a homely affection for the warm security of the tent, and reluctantly wormed out of my bag to face the prospect of lighting the stove. It had snowed a little during the night, and the grass crunched frostily under my feet as I padded over to the cooking rock. There was no sign of Richard stirring as I passed his tiny one-man tent, half collapsed and whitened with hoar frost.

Squatting under the lee of the huge overhanging boulder that had become our kitchen, I relished this moment when I could be entirely alone. I fiddled with the petrol stove which was mulishly objecting to both the temperature and the rusty petrol with which I had filled it. I resorted to brutal coercion when coaxing failed and sat it atop a propane gas stove going full blast. It burst into vigorous life, spluttering out two-foot-high flames in petulant revolt against the dirty petrol.

As the pan of water slowly heated, I looked around at the wide, dry and rock-strewn river bed, the erratic boulder under which I crouched marking the site at a distance in all but the very worst weather. A huge, almost vertical wall of ice and snow soared upwards to the summit of Cerro Sarapo directly in front of the camp, no more than a mile and a half away. Rising from the sea of moraine to my left, two spectacular and extravagant castles of sugar icing, Yerupaja and Rasac, dominated the camp site. The majestic 21,000-foot Siula Grande lay behind Sarapo and was not visible. It had been climbed for the first time in 1936 by two bold Germans via the North Ridge. There had been few ascents since then, and the true prize, the daunting 4,500-foot West Face had so far defeated all attempts.

I turned off the stove and gingerly slopped the water into three large mugs. The sun hadn't cleared the ridge of mountains opposite and it was still chilly in the shadows.

'There's a brew ready, if you're still alive in there,' I announced cheerfully.

I gave Richard's tent a good kicking to knock off the frost and he crawled out looking cramped and cold. Without a word he headed straight for the river bed, clutching a roll of toilet paper.

'Are you still bad?' I asked when he returned.

'Well, I'm not the full ticket but I reckon I'm over the worst. It was bloody freezing last night.'

I wondered if it was the altitude rather than the kidney-bean stew that was getting to him. Our tents were pitched at 15,000 feet, and he was no mountaineer.

Simon and I had found Richard resting in a sleazy hotel in Lima, halfway through his six-month exploration of South America. His wire-rimmed glasses, neat practical clothing and bird-like mannerisms hid a dry humour and a wild repertoire of beachcombing reminiscences. He had lived off grubs and berries with pygmies while dug-out canoeing through the rain forests of Zaire, and had watched a shoplifter being kicked to death in a Nairobi market. His travelling companion was shot dead by trigger-happy soldiers in Uganda for no more than a dubious exchange of cassette tapes.

He travelled the world between bouts of hard work to raise funds. Usually he journeyed alone to see where chance encounters in alien countries would take him. There were distinct advantages, we thought, to having an entertaining watchman in camp to keep an eye on the gear while Simon and I were out climbing. It was probably a gross injustice to the poor hill farmers in this remote spot, but in the backstreets of Lima we had become suspicious of everyone. Anyway, we had invited Richard to come up and join us for a few days if he wanted to see the Andes at close quarters.

It had been two days' walk from where the bone-shaking bus deposited us after 80 heart-stopping miles up the mountain valleys. Forty-six people were crammed into a ramshackle vehicle designed to carry twenty-two, and we were not fortified by the sight of so many wayside shrines to dead bus drivers and their passengers. The engine was held together with nylon string and a flat tyre was changed with a pick-axe.

By the end of the second day, Richard was feeling the effects of altitude. Dusk was gathering as we approached the head of the valley, and he urged Simon and me to go ahead with the donkeys and prepare camp before dark; he would take his time to follow. The way was straightforward now – he couldn't go wrong, he had said.

Slowly he staggered up the treacherous moraines to the lake where he thought we were camped and then remembered a second lake on the map. It had begun to rain and grew increasingly cold. A thin shirt and light cotton trousers were poor protection from a chill Andean night. Tired out, he had descended to the valley in search of shelter. On the way up he had noticed some dilapidated stone and corrugated-iron huts which he assumed to be empty but sufficiently sheltered for a night's rest. He was surprised to find them occupied by two teenage girls and a large brood of children.

After protracted negotiation, he managed to get a place to sleep in the adjoining pigsty. They gave him some boiled potatoes and cheese to eat, and threw in a bundle of moth-eaten sheepskins for warmth. It was a long cold night, and the high-altitude lice enjoyed their best feed for a long time.

Simon came over to the cooking rock and regaled us with a vivid dream. He was firmly convinced that these weird hallucinations were a direct result of the sleeping pills he was taking. I resolved to try some that very night.

I swallowed the last of my coffee as Simon took control of the breakfast-making and then started to write in my diary:

19 May 1985. Base camp. Heavy frost last night, clear skies this morning. I'm still trying to adjust to being here. It feels menacingly remote and exhilarating at the same time; so much better than the Alps – no hordes of climbers, no helicopters, no rescue – just us and the mountains . . . Life seems far simpler and more real here. It's easy to let events and emotions flow past without stopping to look . . .

I wondered how much of this I really believed, and how it related to what we were doing in the Andes. Tomorrow we would start an acclimatisation climb up Rosario Norte. If fit enough at the end of ten days, we would attempt the unclimbed West Face of Siula Grande.

Simon handed me a bowl of porridge and more coffee:

'Shall we go tomorrow then?'

'Might as well. I can't see that it will take us very long if we go light. Could be back down by early afternoon.'

'My only worry is this weather. I'm not sure what it means.'

It had been the same every day since our arrival. The mornings would dawn fine and clear, but by midday banks of cumulus would move in from the east, followed by the inevitable rain. On the high slopes this came as heavy snowfall, and the risk of avalanches and lines of retreat cut off would suddenly become a reality. When such clouds massed in the Alps, retreat was always instantly considered. These weather patterns were different somehow.

'You know, I don't reckon it's anything like as bad as it seems,' Simon suggested thoughtfully. 'Look at yesterday. It clouded in and snowed, but the temperature didn't fall dramatically, there was no lightning or thunder, and there didn't appear to be any desperately high winds on the summits. I don't think these are storms at all.'

Simon could be right, but something was nagging at me, making me question him. 'Are you suggesting we should just climb on through a snowfall? If we do that, won't we run the risk of mistaking a serious storm for the normal pattern?'

'Well, yes, that is a risk. We'll just have to see how it goes. We're certainly not going to learn anything by sitting down here all the time.'

'Right! I was just being cautious about avalanches, that's all.'

Simon laughed. 'Yeah, well, you have good reason to be. Still you survived the last one. I reckon it will be more like the Alps in winter, all powder snow and spindrift, and no big wet snow avalanches. We'll just have to see.'

I envied Simon his carefree take-it-as-it-comes attitude. He had the force to take what was his for the taking, and the freedom of spirit to enjoy it without grumbling worries and doubts. He laughed more often than he grimaced, grinning at his own misfortune as readily as he did at other people's. Tall and powerfully built, he possessed most of life's advantages and few of the drawbacks. He was an easy friend: dependable, sincere, ready to see life as a joke. He had a thatch of blond hair, blue, blue laughing eyes, and that touch of madness which makes just a few people so special. I was glad that we

19

had chosen to come here as a two-man team. There were few other people I could have coped with for so long. Simon was everything that I was not, everything I would like to have been.

'What time do you reckon you'll be back?' Richard asked dozily from his sleeping bag as Simon and I prepared to set off next morning.

'Three o'clock at the latest. We're not intending to spend long over it, and certainly not if the weather breaks again.'

'Okay. Good luck.'

The early-morning frost had hardened the loose ground and the going was easier than we anticipated. It wasn't long before we fell into a steady silent rhythm, zigzagging steadily up the screes. The tents became smaller each time I glanced back, and I began to enjoy the exercise, feeling fitter and stronger than I had thought I would. We were making fast progress despite the altitude, and Simon was keeping to a steady pace that matched mine. I had worried unduly about whether there would be a marked difference between us. If a climber has to slow his natural pace to that of his companion, the unfit climber will soon find himself struggling to keep up. I could imagine the frustrations and tensions that would arise from such a situation.

'How's it going?' I asked when we paused for a short rest.

'I feel pretty good, but I'm glad we're not smoking on this trip.'

I silently agreed, despite all my earlier protests at Simon's suggestion that we should take no cigarettes to base camp. I could feel my lungs working hard in the thin cold air. Heavy smoking had never affected my performance in the Alps, but I was forced to agree that it might be wise to stop during this expedition. The risks of high-altitude sickness and pulmonary oedemas, about which we had heard so much, were all that helped me through a rough few days craving tobacco.

It took a couple of hours to put the scree slopes behind us. Then we headed north towards a high col above an area of broken rock buttresses. The camp disappeared from view and immediately I became aware of the silence and the solitude of our position. For the first time in my life I knew what it meant to be isolated from people and society. It was wonderfully calming and tranquil to be here. I became aware of a feeling of complete freedom – to do what I wanted to do when I wanted to, and in whatever manner. Suddenly the whole day had changed. All lethargy was swept away by an invigorating independence. We had responsibilities to no one but ourselves now, and there would be no one to intrude or come to our rescue . . .

Simon was some distance ahead, quietly climbing, steadily gaining ground. Although he had stolen a march on my less methodical pace, I was no longer concerned about speed and fitness since I knew now that we were pretty evenly matched. I was not in any hurry, and knew we could both reach the summit easily. If a fine viewing point presented itself, I was happy to stop for a moment to take in the view.

The rocky gullies were loose and crumbling. As I emerged from behind a yellow outcrop, I was pleased to see Simon settled down on a col a couple of hundred feet away preparing a hot drink.

'The loose stuff wasn't as bad as I thought it was going to be,' I said a little breathlessly. 'But I could do with that brew.'

'Seen Siula Grande, just over there, left of Sarapo?'

'God, it's fantastic.' I was a little awed by the sight in front of me. 'It's far bigger than those photographs suggested.'

Simon handed me a steaming mug as I sat on my rucksack and gazed at the whole range laid out before us. To my left I could see the South Face of Rasac, a sweeping ice slope with rock bands crossing it, giving it a sort of stripy marbled effect. To the right of Rasac's snowy summit, and connected to it by a dangerously corniced ridge, I could see the slightly lower summit of Seria Norte. From there the corniced ridge dipped down to a saddle before curving up in a huge sweep over two shoulders of rock to the final summit pyramid of Yerupaja. It was by far the highest mountain to be seen and dominated our view as it reared, glistening with ice and fresh snow, high above the Siula glacier. Its South Face formed the classic triangular mountain shape; the West Ridge, corniced and rocky, arched up from the col below Seria Norte, the East Ridge curling round and dropping towards another col. The face below this ridge was an astonishing series of parallel powder-snow flutings etched like lace ribbons in the shadows cast by the sun.

At the base of the ridge I recognised the Santa Rosa col which we had seen in our photographs of Siula Grande. It formed the junction between Yerupaja's South-East Ridge and the start of Siula Grande's North Ridge. This ridge looked relatively uncomplicated where it began to climb up before narrowing and twisting in frighteningly thin edges of snowy cornice and flutings which hung precariously over the edge of the huge West Face. It peaked on the huge snow mushroom that formed the summit of Siula Grande.

That West Face was our ambition. At first it looked confusing, as if I hadn't seen it before. The scale, and the fact that I was looking at it from a different angle from that shown in the photographs, made it unrecognisable until gradually distinctive features fell into place. A huge bank of cumulus was beginning to spill up over the North Ridge of Siula Grande, as always moving in from the east where the huge rain forests of the Amazon basin, heated up in the day's sun, pushed out these regular banks of moisture-laden clouds.

'I think you're right about the weather, Simon,' I said. 'That's not storm weather at all. I'll bet it's just a convection system coming off the jungle.'

'Yeah, just getting up our normal afternoon dousing.'

'How high do you think we are now?' I asked.

'Must be about 18,000 feet, perhaps a bit more. Why?'

'Well, it's a height record for both of us, and we seem hardly to have noticed.'

'When you're sleeping at about the same height as Mont Blanc it doesn't seem very significant, does it?' Simon said with a mischievous grin.

By the time we had finished our drinks the first wet snowflakes were beginning to fall. The summit of Rosario was still clear, though it wouldn't be for very much longer. It was probably no more than 400 feet higher than our position on the col, and in clear weather could have been reached in little over an hour. Neither of us said anything about going straight down. It was an unspoken understanding between us that the summit would be left out this time.

Simon shouldered his pack and set off down towards the top of the scree slopes. He began to run and slide down the rocky gullies we had struggled up. Then we whooped and howled our way headlong down 1,500 feet of loose sliding screes, attempting to execute boots-together ski-turns, and arrived back at camp exhilarated and panting.

Richard had started to prepare the evening meal and handed us the mugs of tea he had made when he spotted us high on the screes. We sat by the roaring petrol stoves to tell him in rambling excited bursts what we had done and seen, until the rain came on up the valley in sudden waves and drove us into the shelter of the large dome tent.

After it grew dark at about six-thirty, anyone approaching the tent would have seen only a warm candlelight glowing red and green through the tent fabric and heard a quiet murmuring of conversation, punctuated now and then by gusts of ribald laughter as Richard told a hilarious story about eight members of a New Zealand rugby team lost in the jungles of central Africa. We planned our future training climbs before playing cards long into the night.

Our next objective was to be the unclimbed South Ridge of Cerro Yantauri, only a short walk across the river bed from our tents. Indeed it looked as if we would be in sight of camp all the way to the summit. The South Ridge ran from right to left up early rocky outcrops before forming a long and elegant corniced snow ridge which led to a highly unstable area of seracs that mushroomed to the summit. We would bivouac high on the ridge, either on the way up or on the descent, to test out our theories about the weather.

The morning was cold and sunny, but an unusually menacing look in the sky in the east persuaded us to leave the South Ridge of Yantauri for another day. Simon went for a bath and shave in a near-by ice-melt pool while I set off with Richard to see whether we could buy milk and cheese from the girls at the huts.

They seemed pleased to see us and were delighted to sell us their homemade cheese. Through Richard's halting Spanish, we discovered that their names were Gloria and Norma, and that they slept in the huts when they brought their father's cattle up to the high pastures. They had a wild, abandoned look about them, but they took great care of the little children, who seemed perfectly well able to look after themselves. We idled in the sun, watching them at work. Three-year-old Alecia (whom I had nicknamed Paddington) guarded the entrance to the cattle enclosure, preventing the cows and calves from escaping, while her brothers and sisters milked, or held back the calves from suckling, or prepared the whey in muslin bags. Everything was done with laughter at an unhurried happy pace. We arranged for Gloria's brother Spinoza to bring us supplies from the nearest village in the next few days and returned to camp nibbling on the cheese, keeping a wary eye on the clouds, which were about to empty their loads earlier than usual. The prospect of fresh vegetables, eggs, bread and fruit was almost too much to contemplate after two weeks on a monotonous diet of pasta and beans.

The next day we left the camp early for Yantauri. It was an inauspicious start. The screes proved highly dangerous, with stone-falls smacking down on them from high on the rubble-strewn West Face above us. We were nervous and jittery, and wanted to move fast, but our heavy sacks dictated otherwise. Half-way up the lower screes Simon realised he had left his camera down where he had last rested. He dumped his sack and ran back down while I carried on upwards to the right, heading for the protection of the lower rock walls.

By six o'clock that evening we were established high on the ridge, but the weather had taken a turn for the worse and dark threatening clouds were rapidly converging on our exposed position. As darkness fell we erected our little bivi tent against a small sheltered rock wall and settled down anxiously to sleep. It snowed steadily through the night but the feared storm did not materialise. Our weather theory seemed to be borne out.

We started up the snowy South Ridge in high hopes next morning, but at 18,000 feet we were forced to give up the struggle. Waist-deep powder snow had reduced us to an exhausted wallowing. The heavily corniced ridge would be far too dangerous. When I plunged through a fissure splitting a double cornice below the summit seracs and could see clear down the West Face we decided to call it a day.

Tired out, we returned to the tents after a trying descent of the loose rubble-strewn walls of the West Face. At least now we had some vital answers about the weather. Doubtless there would be serious storms at times, but at least we wouldn't have to retreat at the first sign of cloud build-up.

Two days later we set off again, this time for the South Ridge of Seria Norte. It looked spectacular from base camp, and as far as we knew it had never been climbed. As we drew closer we began to see why. Back home in Sheffield Al Rouse had told us that this was 'a ridge of some difficulty'. On close inspection we realised that Al's reputation for understatement was wholly justified. After a cold and cramped bivouac, we again sloughed up exhausting powder snow to reach a high col at the foot of the ridge. An astonishing series of cornices protruding almost vertically from the ridge leapfrogged 2,000 feet above us to the summit. To have touched the bottom cornice with an ice axe would have brought the whole mass of tottering ice tumbling down on to our heads. We managed to laugh at the waste of effort and wondered what Richard would think of our third failure to reach a summit. But we were fit, acclimatised and ready now for our main objective – the West Face of Siula Grande.

For two whole days we gorged ourselves on food and sunshine, preparing for the West Face. I began to feel spasms of fear now that we were committed to Siula in the next fine-weather window. What if something went wrong? It wouldn't take much to kill us off. I saw how very much alone we had chosen to be and felt small. Simon chuckled when I mentioned my worries. He knew the cause, and probably felt the same tension inside. It was healthy to be a little scared, and good to sense my body responding to the fear. We can do it, we can do it ... I kept repeating like a mantra whenever I felt that hollow hungry gap in my stomach. It wasn't false bravado. Psyching up for it, getting ready to make the final move, was always a difficult part of preparation for me. Rationalisation, some people called it – bloody frightened seemed a better description, and more honest!

'Okay,' Simon said finally, 'we snow-hole at the foot of the face, then go in one push the next day. Two days up, two days down, I reckon.'

'If the weather holds ...'

In the morning the outlook was bleak. Clouds hid the peaks and only their flanks were visible beneath a murky ceiling. There was an odd sense of menace in the air. We both noticed it as we packed our rucksacks in readiness for an early start the following day should the weather change. Was this to be a full-bore storm or simply an earlier than usual present from the Amazon? I pushed an extra cylinder of gas into my sack.

'I wouldn't mind winning the next one. So far it's mountains three, climbers nil.'

I smiled at Simon's rueful expression.

'It'll be different on Siula. For a start it's too bloody steep to hold much powder.'

'Four days you reckon, then,' Richard repeated casually.

'Five at the outside' – Simon glanced at me – 'and if we're not back after a week you'll be the proud owner of all our gear!'

I could see that Richard laughed only because we laughed. I didn't envy him the wait, never knowing what might be happening up there. Five days is a very long time, especially on your own with no one to talk to.

'You'll probably be jumping to all sorts of conclusions after three days, but try not to worry. We know what we're doing, and if something goes wrong there is nothing whatever you can do.'

Despite all our efforts to cut down on weight, the rucksacks were going to be a heavy burden. We were taking a much larger selection of hardware than before. The bivi tent was far too cumbersome; we decided to leave it behind and rely on finding good snow holes instead. Even without the tent, the snow stakes, ice screws, crampons and axes, rock gear, stoves, gas, food and sleeping bags all amounted to a daunting load.

Richard had decided to accompany us as far as the glacier, and we got away next morning at a steady pace under a hot sun. After an hour we reached the beginning of the glacier and started up a steep gully between the lower glacier moraines and a shield of ice-worn rock that formed the left bank of the glacier. Mud and rubble gave way to a jumble of boulders and scree. It was awkward scrambling round and over these obstacles, some of which were many times the size of a man, and it was all the more difficult with large sacks on our backs. Richard kept up well after two weeks at high altitude but a bristling series of ice spikes and mud-smeared glacier ice, visible from where we rested, presented a formidable obstacle to him in lightweight walking shoes. To get past, and up on to the glacier, we would have to negotiate a short, steep, ice cliff some 80 to 100 feet high. Large rocks were balanced precariously above the line of ascent.

'I don't think you should come any further,' Simon said. 'We could get you up there, but not back again.'

Richard looked around ruefully at the barren view of mud and perched boulders. He had been hoping for something more impressive than this. The West Face of Siula was not yet in view.

'I'll take your pictures before you go,' he announced. 'You never know, I might make a fortune selling them as obituary photos!'

'Much appreciated, I'm sure!' Simon muttered.

We left him there among the boulders. From our position high above on the ice cliffs he looked forlornly abandoned. He was in for a lonely time.

'Take care!' wafted up to us from cupped hands below.

'Don't worry,' Simon shouted, 'we don't intend sticking our necks out. We'll be back in time. See you . . .'

The lonely figure was soon lost amid the boulders as we headed up towards the first crevasses, where we put on our crampons and roped up. The heat of the glacier was intense under the glare reflected from icy mountain walls. There was not a breath of wind. The glacier edge was cracked and contorted, and we looked back at our route so as to fix the features in our minds. Neither of us wanted to forget it on the way down. Our tracks would certainly have disappeared under fresh snow by then, and it was important to know whether to go below or above the crevasses when we returned.

As a cold clear night came over the mountains we were cosily ensconced in our snow hole beneath the face. It would be a freezing early-morning start tomorrow.

2

TEMPTING FATE

It was cold. Five-in-the-morning cold, on a high Andean glacier. I struggled with zips and gaiters until my fingers would not work, and I rocked back and forward, hands in my crotch, moaning with the hot aches. It had never been this bad before, I thought, as the pain in my fingers fired up, but then I always thought that with hot aches. So damned painful.

Simon grinned at my agony. I knew that once warmed up I wouldn't get the aches again. It was some consolation.

'I'll go first, shall I?' Simon said, knowing he had me at a disadvantage. I nodded miserably, and he set off up the avalanche cone above our snow hole towards the icefield which reared up in blue early-morning ice.

Right then, this was it! I looked at Simon leaning above the small crevasse at the base of the face and planting his ice axe firmly into the steep ice wall above. The weather looked perfect. No tell-tale cloud front running a storm this time. If it held we'd be up and half-way down before the next bad spell.

I stamped my feet, trying to get my boots warmed up. Fragments of ice tinkled down on to my shoulders as Simon hammered axes up the ice, bunny-hopping his feet, then axes in again. I ducked from the cold shower, looking away to the south at the sky lightening by the minute above the summit of Sarapo.

When I next looked up Simon was nearly at the end of the rope, 150 feet above me. I had to crane my neck to see him. It was very steep.

Following his cheery shout I sorted out my axes, checked my crampons, and started up towards the wall. As I reached the crevasse I realised how precipitously steep it was. I felt off balance, forced out by the angle, until I had hauled myself out over the lip of the crevasse and up on to the ice wall. Stiff and unco-ordinated at first, I struggled unnecessarily until, warmed by the effort, my body began to flow into rhythmic movements, and a rush of exultation at being here set me off up towards the distant figure.

Simon stood on the outside of one foot, hanging back on the ice screws hammered into the ice, casual, relaxed:

'Steep, isn't it?'

'Almost vertical, that bit at the bottom,' I replied, 'but the ice is brilliant! I'll bet this is steeper than the Droites.'

Simon gave me the remaining screws and I carried on above him, sweating now, the morning cold driven off. Head down, keep looking at your feet, swing, swing, hop, look at your feet, swing swing ... all the way up a smooth 150 feet, no effort, no headache, feeling on top of the world. I drove in the screws, seeing the ice crack, split and protest – drive in, solid, clip in, lean back, relax. This was it!

I felt the flow, the heat and blood and strength flowing. It was right. 'Yeeee haaaaaaaa!' – listen to that echo, round and round the glacier. Thin wandering footprints, shadow lines, could be seen twisting up from the darker shadow of the collapsed snow hole on the glacier, already a long way down.

Simon was coming up, hitting hard, ice splintering down below him, hitting hard and strong, walking up on points of steel, head down, hitting, hopping, on past me and up, without a word, just hitting hard, breathing steady, getting smaller.

We climbed higher, 1,000 feet, 2,000, until we wondered when this icefield would end, and the rhythm became ragged with the monotony. We kept looking up and to our right, following the line we had chosen – a line that now looked different with the shortened perspective. The rock buttress swept up beside us into tangled gullies. Ribboned snow on the ledges, ice weeps and icicles everywhere, but where was the gully we wanted?

The sun was fully up; jackets and tops were in the sacks. Following Simon, I was slowing with the heat, dry-mouthed, wanting a drink. The angle eased. Looking to my right, I smiled seeing Simon with legs astride a large rock, sack off, taking a photograph of me as I came over the top edge of the icefield and headed towards him on an easy ramp line.

'Lunch,' he said, passing me a chocolate bar and some prunes. The gas stove hissed away busily, sheltered by his rucksack. 'The brew's nearly ready.'

I sat back, glad to rest in the sun and look around. It was past noon, and warm. Ice clattered down from the headwall which reared 2,000 feet above us. For the moment we were safe. The rock on which we lunched topped a slight rib, splitting the ground above the icefield so that the debris tumbled harmlessly past on either side. We sat, perched above the icefield, which was steeply sloped, dropping like a vertical wall beneath our lunch rock. A giddy, dragging sensation urged me to lean further out over the drop, pulling me down at the snow-ice sweeping away below. Looming over, with my stomach clenched, and a sharp strong sense of danger, I enjoyed the feeling.

Our footsteps and the snow hole were no longer visible, lost in the dazzling blur of white ice and white glacier. With the wind tonight all signs of our passing would be gone.

The upper tiers of the great yellow rock buttress which split the face crowded out our view of the way ahead. As we climbed up parallel with it, we began to see just how big it was – a respectable 1,000-foot-high wall which would have been a mountain in itself in the Dolomites. Stones had whirred down from the upper reaches all day, smacking into the right side of the icefield, then bouncing and wheeling down to the glacier. Thank God we hadn't climbed any nearer to the buttress! From a distance the stones seemed small and harmless, but the smallest, falling free from many hundreds of feet above, would have hurt us as surely as any rifle bullet.

We had to find the steep ice couloir which ran up through the side of this buttress, and would eventually lead us into the wide hanging gully we had seen from Seria Norte. This would be the key to the climb. We had under six hours to find it, climb it, and dig a comfortable snow cave in the gully above. A large ice cliff hung out from the edge of the hanging gully, streaming twenty- to thirty-foot icicles – free-hanging above the 200-foot wall below. That was what we wanted to get into, but it would be impossible to go directly up the wall through the fringe of icicles.

'How much higher do you reckon the couloir is?' I asked, seeing that Simon was examining the rocks intently.

'We'll have to go higher,' he said. 'It can't be that one.' He pointed to an extremely steep cascade of icicles just left of the ice cliff.

'It might go, but it isn't the one we saw. You're right, it's above that mixed ground.'

We wasted no more time. I put the stove away, and sorted out ice screws and axes before I led off, crossing the ramp, and then front-pointing up steepening water ice. The ice was harder and more brittle. I could see Simon, when I looked between my feet, ducking away from large chunks of ice that were breaking away from my axes. I heard his curses as some big pieces made painful direct hits.

Simon joined me at the belay and told me what he thought of my bombardment.

'Well, it's my turn now.'

He carried on up, following a slanting line to the right over bulges and areas of thin ice which showed the rock bared in places. I ducked away from some heavy ice fall, then more, before a warning doubt clicked in my head. Simon was above me, but off to the right! I looked up to see where the ice was coming from and saw the corniced summit ridge far above me. Some of the cornices overhung the West Face by as much as forty feet, and we were directly under their fall-line. Suddenly the day seemed less casual and relaxed. I watched Simon's progress, now agonisingly slow and hunched up, my hair bristling at the thought of a cornice collapse. I followed him as fast as I could. He too had realised the danger.

'Christ! Let's get out of here,' he said, passing me the ice screws.

I set off hurriedly. A cascade of ice dropped over steep underlying rocks in a fifty-foot step. I could see it was steep, 80° maybe, and hammered in a screw when I reached its base. I would climb it in one push, then move right.

Water was running under the ice, and in places the rock sparked as my axe hit it. I slowed down, climbing carefully, cautious of rushing into a mistake. Holding on to my left axe near the top of the cascade, I tiptoed out on my front points. Halfway into swinging my right axe, a sudden dark object rushed at me.

'Rocks!' I yelled, ducking down and away. Heavy blows thudded into my shoulder, whacking against my sack, and then it was past, and I watched Simon looking straight up at my warning. The boulder, about four-foot square, swept below me directly at him. It seemed an age before he reacted, and when he did it was with a slow-motion casualness which I found hard to believe. He leaned to his left and dropped his head as the heavy stone seemed to hit him full-on. I shut my eyes, and hunched harder as more stones hit me. When I looked again, Simon was all but hidden beneath the sack which he had swept up over his head.

'You okay?'

'Yes!' he shouted from behind his sack.

'I thought you were hit.'

'Only by small stuff. Get moving, I don't like it here.'

I climbed the last few feet of the cascade, and moved quickly right to the shelter of the rock. Simon grinned when he reached me:

'Where did that lot come from?'

'I don't know. I only saw it at the last moment. Too bloody close!'

'Let's get on. I can see the gully from here.'

Boosted with adrenalin, he climbed quickly towards the steep icy couloir visible in a corner of the main buttress. It was four-thirty. We had an hour and a half of light left.

I went on past his stance for another full rope length but the couloir seemed no nearer. The flat, white light made it hard to gauge distances. Simon set out on the last short pitch to the foot of the couloir.

'We ought to bivi here,' I said. 'It will be dark soon.'

'Yeah, but there's no chance of a snow hole, or any ledges.'

I could see he was right. Any night spent here would be uncomfortable. It was already getting hard to see.

'I'll try and get up this before dark.'

'Too late . . . it *is* dark!'

'Well, I bloody hope we can do it in one rope length then.' I didn't like the prospect of blundering around on steep ice in the dark trying to sort out belays.

I made a short traverse left to the foot of the couloir. 'Jesus! This is overhanging, and the ice is terrible!'

Simon said nothing.

Twenty feet of rotten honeycombed ice reared up in front of me, but above that I could see it relented and lay back to a more reasonable angle. I banged an ice screw into the good water ice at the foot of the wall, clipped the rope through it, turned my head-torch on, took a deep breath, and started climbing.

I was nervous at first for the angle forced me backwards, and the honeycombs crunched and sharded away beneath my feet, but the axes, biting deeper into harder ice, were solid and soon I was engrossed. A short panting struggle and the wall was beneath me, Simon no longer in sight. I stood on tiptoe on glassy hard water ice, blue in my torchlight, curving up above me into shadows.

The dark night silence was broken only by my axe blows and the wavering cone of light from my torch. The climbing held me completely, so that Simon might as well not have been there.

Hit hard. Hit again – that's it, now the hammer. Look at your feet. Can't see them. Kick hard, and again. On up, peering into shadows, trying to make out the line. The blue glass curves left, like a bob-sleigh run, the angle steepening under a huge fringe of icicles on the right. Is that another way up, behind the icicles? I move up, under the ice fringe. A few icicles break away, and thump tinkle down, chandelier sounds in the dark, and a muffled shout echoes up to me from below – no time to answer. This way is wrong. Damn, damn! Get back down, reverse it. No! Put a screw in.

I fumble at my harness for a screw but can't find one – forget it, just get back below the icicles.

I shouted down to Simon when I reached the couloir again, but I couldn't hear his reply. Spindrift powder rushed down in a burst from above. Unexpected, it made my heart leap.

I had no ice screws. I had forgotten to take them from Simon and had used my only screw down at the bottom. I did not know what to do, 120 feet up very steep ice. Go back down? I was scared of the unprotected drop beneath me, and of the idea of needing an ice screw for a belay if I couldn't find any rock. I shouted again but there was no reply. Take a few breaths and get on with it!

I could see the top of the couloir fifteen feet above me, the last ten feet rearing up steeply, tube-shaped, the good ice giving way to mushy powder. I bridged across the tube, legs splayed against yielding snow. I flailed my axes, dreading the 240-foot fall below me on to one ice screw, and thrashed about me, breathing quick, frightened gasps of effort before I could pull myself out on to the easy snow slopes above the couloir.

When I had regained my breath, I climbed up to a rock wall and arranged a belay in the loose cracks and blocks.

Simon joined me, breathing hard. 'You took your time,' he snapped.

I bristled. 'It was bloody hard, and I was as good as soloing it. I had no screws with me.'

'Forget it. Let's find a bivi.'

It was ten o'clock, and the wind had got up, making the minus-fifteen temperature seem a lot colder. Tired and irritable after a hard fifteen-hour day, we had dreaded the hour or so it would take us to dig a snow hole.

'Nothing doing here,' I said, eyeing the slope critically. 'Not deep enough to dig.'

'I could try that dollop up there.'

Simon indicated a huge golf-ball of snow, fifty feet across, which clung defiantly to the vertical rock wall thirty feet above us. He moved up to it and cautiously started prodding it with his axe. On my shaky belay, I appreciated his caution, for I would be swept away if it suddenly parted company with the wall.

'Joe!' Simon yelled. 'Wow! You're not going to believe this.' I heard a piton being hammered into rock, and a few more squeaks of joy, and then the call to come up to him.

I felt dubious, and gingerly poked my head through the small hole Simon had made.

'Good God!'

'I said you wouldn't believe it.' Simon sat back comfortably on his sack, belayed to a good strong peg, and waved regally at his new domain. 'And it has a bathroom,' he said with glee, all tiredness and bad humour gone.

The snow was hollow. Inside there was one large chamber, almost high enough to stand in, and beside it another smaller cave. Here was a ready-made palace!

Yet, as we got organised and settled into our sleeping bags, I could not help turning over in my head my usual dislike of bivi sites, trying to assess the safety margin. I had good reason to be alarmed about the precarious state of this one, and Simon knew why, but there was no point in harping on about it. There was nowhere else.

There had been no alternative, as I remembered all too vividly, two years earlier when climbing on the Bonatti Pillar on the south-west side of Les Petits Drus. I was elated to have made such fast progress with Ian Whittaker up the 2,000-foot golden-red granite spire which dominates the view from the Chamonix valley. The architectural magnificence of its lines drawn sharply by the shadows of the sun against the softer backdrop of the whole range of the French Alps had made this climb one of the most aesthetically pleasing routes in the Alps. We had climbed well that day to establish ourselves by nightfall just a few hundred feet from the summit, though still on very steep and difficult ground. There was no possibility of reaching the top that night, nor was there need for haste in seeking a ledge on which to sleep, for the weather was clear and settled, and we would certainly reach the top the following day. It would be another warm night, and this high up, at 12,000 feet, the sky would be brilliant with stars.

Ian had climbed above my small stance overlooking the airy sweep of the precipitous walls below. The corner he was following was relentlessly steep and failing light made him painfully slow. I waited, shivering in the chill evening air, hopping from foot to foot, trying to regain circulation despite my cramped position. I was tired after the long day and yearned to lie back and rest in comfort.

At last a muffled shout told me he had found something, and soon I was cursing and struggling in the gathering dusk up the corner Ian had just led. Even before it had darkened I had spotted that we were slightly off route. We had climbed directly up a steep crack splitting a vertical wall instead of traversing to the right. This had placed us beneath a huge overhang about 150 feet above us. No doubt we would have to resort to complicated diagonal abseiling in the morning to get past it. For now, it had its advantages: at least we would be protected from any rockfall during the night.

I found Ian sitting on a ledge about four feet wide but long enough for the two of us to lie down foot-to-head. It would be quite adequate for a night's sleep. As I climbed up to him I noticed in my torchlight that the ledge was in fact the top of a large pedestal fixed to the vertical wall above the corner we had just climbed. It was solid and gave us no reason to think it might be unsafe.

An hour later we had fixed a handrail safety rope, strung between an old ring peg and a spike of rock, clipped ourselves in and settled down to sleep.

The next few seconds were unforgettable.

I was inside a protective waterproof bivouac bag, half-asleep, and Ian was making final adjustments to his safety line. Suddenly and without warning, I felt myself drop swiftly. Simultaneously there was an ear-splitting roar and grinding. With my head inside the bag and my arms flailing outside the opening at my chest I knew nothing except the sickening dread as I went plummeting down into the 2,000-foot abyss below. I heard a high-pitched yelp of fear amid the heavy roaring, then felt a springy recoil. The safety rope had held. All my weight was held on my armpits, as I had accidentally caught the safety rope in the fall. I swung gently on the rope, trying to remember whether I had tied-in to the rope and gripping my arms tight just in case.

The thunderous sound of tons of granite plunging down the pillar echoed and then died to silence.

I was completely disorientated. The silence seemed frighteningly ominous. Where was Ian? I thought of that fleeting yelp, and was horrified by the idea that perhaps he had not tied-on after all.

'By 'eck!' I heard close by in gruff Lancastrian.

I struggled to get my head out of the tightly squeezed bag. Ian was hanging beside me on the V-shaped safety rope. His head was lolling on his chest, his head-torch casting a yellow glow on to the surrounding rock. I could see blood on his neck.

I fumbled inside my bag for my head-torch, and then, carefully lifting the elastic torch strap from his blood-matted hair, I examined his injury. He had trouble talking at first, for he had hit his head hard in the fall. Fortunately the cut was a minor one, but the shock of the fall, while half-asleep in the dark, had completely confused us. It took some time to realise that the whole pedestal had detached itself from the pillar and dropped straight off the mountain face. There was a good deal of nervous swearing and hysterical giggling as, gradually, we became aware of the seriousness of our position.

At last, we fell silent. A terrible fear and insecurity had overtaken our boisterous reaction to the unimaginable event. Shining torches below, we saw the remains of our two ropes, which had been hanging beneath the ledge. They were cut to pieces, shredded by the falling rock. Turning round to inspect the safety line, we were appalled to find that the old ring peg on which we hung was moving, and that the spike of rock had been badly damaged. It looked as if one of the two attachment points would give way at any moment. We knew that if just one anchor point failed we would both be hurled into the void. We quickly searched for our equipment to see how we might improve the anchors, only to find that all of it, including our boots, had fallen with the ledge. So confident had we been in the safety of the ledge that we hadn't thought it necessary to clip our gear to the rope. We could do nothing.

To attempt to climb up or down would have been suicidal. The shadow of the huge overhang above us put paid to any idea of climbing in socks without ropes. Beneath stood a vertical wall hidden by the darkness – an obstacle we could descend only on ropes. The nearest ledges were 200 feet below, and we would certainly fall to our deaths long before we got anywhere near them.

We hung on that fragile rope for twelve interminable hours. Eventually our shouts were heard and a rescue helicopter succeeded in plucking us from the wall. The experience of that long, long night, expecting to fall at any time, one minute laughing hysterically, then silence, always with stomachs clenched, petrified, waiting for something we did not wish to think about, will never be forgotten.

Ian returned to the Alps the following summer, but his desire to climb had been destroyed. He returned home vowing never to go to the Alps again. I was lucky, or stupid, and got over my dread – except when it came to bivouacs.

'What shall it be then?' Simon held up two foil bags. 'Moussaka or Turkey Supreme?'

'Who gives a toss! They're both disgusting!'

'Good choice. We'll have the Turkey.'

Two brews of passion fruit and a few prunes later we settled back for sleep.

3

STORM AT THE SUMMIT

Getting organised in the morning was a much easier business than it had been previously. We had the advantage of standing room when it came to rolling up Karrimats, packing sleeping bags, and sorting out the climbing gear that had been dropped in a tangled mess on our arrival the night before.

It was my turn to lead. Simon remained inside the snow cave, belayed to a rock piton, while I gingerly stepped out of the small entrance on to the sloped ice of the gully we had ascended in the dark. The ground was unfamiliar to me. I was standing on good ice which funnelled down into a narrowing curved cone below me before disappearing into the top of the tube which I had struggled so hard to get out of last night. The huge icefield we had climbed yesterday was no longer visible. I looked over to my right. A short distance above me the top of the gully reared up in a vertical cascade of ice, but over on its far side I could see that the angle eased and there was a way up and past the cascade into another gully above.

I tiptoed to the right, stopping to drive in a screw before launching up the side of the cascade. It was excellent water ice and I enjoyed the aggressive warming work. I glanced back at the entrance of the snow cave and saw Simon peeping out, feeding the rope as I climbed. The structure of the natural cave looked even more impressive than it had last night and I couldn't help wondering at our good fortune to have found it, for a night spent in the open at the top of the gully would have been, to say the least, uncomfortable.

Above the cascade I ran out the rest of the rope, following a snowy gully. Simon quickly joined me.

'Just as we thought,' I said. 'We should reach the hanging ramp on the next pitch.'

He set off to the right before disappearing from the minor gully, where I stood resting, into the key ramp line we had seen so long ago on Seria Norte. I reckoned that the main difficulties were now behind us and it would be only a matter of running it out to the top of the ramp, and then up the summit slopes.

When I joined Simon in the ramp I realised that our problems were not over. At the top of the ramp we could see that there was a formidable barrier of tooth-shaped seracs with no apparent way through them. The vertical rock walls on each side of the ramp would be impossibly hard to ascend, and the seracs stretched from wall to wall without a break.

'Damn!'

'Yeah, it's bad news. I wasn't expecting those.'

'There may be an exit,' I said. 'If not, we're stuck.'

'Bloody hope not! It's a long way back.'

I looked at the near-by peaks, trying to gauge our height on the mountain.

'We bivied at five eight hundred metres last night. That's what? Nineteen thousand feet . . . right, that means we have about fifteen hundred to go,' I said.

'Two thousand, more like.'

'Okay, two, but we did at least two and a half thousand on harder ground yesterday so we should top out today.'

'I wouldn't be so sure. Depends on how hard that exit is, and remember the last bit is all flutings.'

I set off up the 55° ramp and made fast progress. We alternated leads, rarely talking to each other, concentrating on forcing the pace. Yesterday we had used ice screws to protect each rope length, and the steep ice had slowed us down. Today we could feel the thin air taking its toll where the easier ground enabled us to climb an almost continuous double pitch, kicking steps up to the leader for 150 feet, and then up past him for the same again.

I was breathing heavily as I dug through the soft surface snow to find the firm ice below. I drove in two ice screws and planted both axes above my stance before tying into them and shouting for Simon to come up. We were close to the serac barrier, having climbed 1,000 feet up the ramp. I checked my watch: one o'clock. We had overslept and made a late start, but, after ten pitches in four and a half hours, we had made up for it. I felt confident and at ease. We were a match for this route and I now knew that we would finish it. I felt a thrill at the knowledge that I was, at last, on the verge of achieving a first ascent, and a hard one at that.

As Simon panted up, the sun crept over the seracs at the top of the ramp and spilled bright white light down the sweep of snow below us. Simon was grinning broadly. I needed no explanation for his good humour. It was one of those moments when everything came together, and there were no struggles or doubts, and nothing more to do but enjoy the sensation.

'May as well get past the seracs and then rest.'

'Sure,' Simon agreed, as he studied the barrier above. 'See those icicles? That's the way past.'

I looked at the cascade of ice and, at first, I dismissed it as too difficult. It was clearly overhanging at the bottom. A leaning wall of smooth blue ice with a huge fringe of icicles dripping from its head provided the only solid surface across the otherwise powdery seracs. Yet, this cascade was the only weakness that I could spot in the barrier. If we were to attempt it, we would have to climb the initial ice wall for some twenty-five feet and then break a way through the icicles and continue up the more reasonably angled cascade ice above.

'It looks hard.'

'Yes. I'd prefer to attempt the rock first.'

'It's loose as hell.'

'I know, but it might go. I'll give it a try anyway.'

He moved some pitons, a few wires, and a couple of 'Friends' round to the front of his harness before edging left to the start of the rock wall. I was anchored firmly, just below and to the right of the cascade. The rock, yellow and crumbly, bordered the vertical powdery snow between the cascade and the rocky side of the ramp.

I watched Simon carefully, for I knew that if he fell it would be with the sudden violence of hand- or foot-holds breaking away and not the gradual surrender to waning strength. He placed the camming device in a crack as high up the wall as he could. It expanded evenly into the crack with each of its four cams pressed hard against the rock. I guessed that it would be the rock which would break away, and not the 'Friend', if Simon fell.

He stepped up cautiously, testing his foot-holds with light kicks, and hitting the holds above his head to check their looseness. He hesitated a moment, stretched against the wall, gripping the rock above him at full reach, and then began to pull himself up slowly. I tensed, holding the ropes locked in the sticht plate, so that I could hold his fall immediately.

Suddenly, the holds tore loose from the wall, and for a second Simon held his poise, his hands still outstretched but now gripping two lumps of loose rock. Then he was off, falling backwards into the gully below. I braced myself, expecting the 'Friend' to rip out as well, but it held firm, and I stopped his short tumble with ease.

'Brilliant!' I said, laughing at the surprise on his face.

'Shit! . . . I was sure those were solid.'

When he had got back to me he looked at the cascade again.

'I don't fancy doing it directly, but if I can get past the right side I should be able to crack it.'

'The ice looks mushy there.'

'We'll see.'

He launched himself up the right side of the cascade, avoiding the steep wall but attempting to make a slight traverse to the right before climbing back left above the icicles. Unfortunately the ice gave way to honeycombed snow and sugary ice crystals. He managed to reach a point parallel with the top of the icicles before the conditions became impossible and he could go no higher. He was twenty feet above me, and for a while it seemed as if he was stuck: reversing what he had just climbed would be to invite a nasty fall. Eventually he succeeded in fixing a sling around a thick icicle which had rejoined the cascade to form a loop, and he abseiled off this down to my stance.

'I'm knackered. You have a go.'

'Okay, but I'd move further to the side if I were you. I'll have to knock most of those icicles away.'

Many of them were as thick as a man's arm and nearly five feet long. Some even bigger. I started up the ice wall, which pushed me back off balance, and at once I felt the strain on my arms. The sack on my back pulled me away from the ice. I bunny-hopped my crampons quickly up the wall, smashing my axes hard into the brittle ice above, pulling up, hopping again – all the time trying to save my strength by climbing fast. As I neared the icicles I realised that I would be unable to hold on for very much longer; already I was too tired to break away the icicles while holding on to the wall with one axe. I swung as hard as I could until my axe bit in deeply, and was firm enough to hold me. I then clipped my harness into the wrist-loop on the axe and hung wearily from it. I kept a wary eye on the axe tip embedded in the ice, and only when I was sure it was holding my full weight safely did I extract my hammer axe from the wall and, reaching above me, hammer an ice screw into the wall.

I clipped the rope through the screw and breathed a sigh of relief. At least there was no longer a danger of falling more than five or six feet. The icicles were within easy reach. Without thinking I swung my hammer through the fringe of ice and, even more stupidly, looked up at what I was doing. The best part of a hundredweight of icicles smashed down on to my head and shoulders and clattered away down on to Simon. We both started swearing. I cursed myself and the sharp pain of a split lip and cracked tooth, and Simon cursed me.

'Sorry . . . didn't think.'

'Yeah. I noticed.'

When I looked up again I saw that although it was painful the hammer had done the trick and there was now a way clear through to the easier-angled ice above. It didn't take long to swarm up the top of the wall and run the remainder of the rope to a belay in the wide shallow gully above.

Simon came up covered in ice particles and frosted white by the powder snow which had swept down the cascade. He carried on past me to a slight ridge which marked the end of the ramp and the start of the summit slopes. He had lit the gas stove and cleared a place to sit in comfort by the time I joined him.

'Your mouth is bleeding,' he said flatly.

'It's nothing. It was my fault anyway.'

It was noticeably colder now that we were away from the shelter of the ice gullies and exposed to a steady breeze. For the first time we could see the summit, formed from a huge overhanging cornice which bulged out over the slopes 800 feet above us. The ridge sweeping off to the left would be our line of descent, but we couldn't see it very well in the swirling clouds which were steadily spilling over from the east. It looked as if bad weather was on the way.

Simon passed me a hot drink and then huddled deeper into his jacket with his back to the bitter wind. He was looking at the summit slopes, searching for the best line of ascent. It was the state of the snow on this last part of the route that worried us more than the angle or the technical difficulties. The whole slope was corrugated by powder flutings which had gradually built up as fresh snow had sloughed down the face. We had heard all about Peruvian flutings and hadn't liked the stories; it was best not to attempt them. The weather patterns in Europe never produced such horrors. South American mountains were renowned for these spectacular snow and ice creations, where powder snow seemed to defy gravity and form 70°, even 80° slopes, and ridges developed into tortured unstable cornices of huge size, built up one on top of the other. On any other mountains the powder would have swept on down and only formed on much easier-angled slopes.

Above us a rock band cut across the whole slope. It was not steep, but was powdered with a treacherous coating of snow. After 100 feet it merged back into the snow slope, which grew steeper as it climbed up. The flutings started shortly above the rock band and continued without break to the summit. Once we had established ourselves in the gully formed between two flutings we would have to force a way to the top, for it would be impossible to traverse out by crossing a fluting and getting into the neighbouring gully. It would be vitally important to choose the right gully, and we could see that many of them closed down into dead-ends as two flutings merged together. If I looked carefully I could make out a few gullies which did not close down, but as soon as I tried to look at the whole slope these became lost in the maze of gullies and flutings streaming down the face.

'Christ! It looks desperate!' Simon said. 'I can't work out a way up at all.'

'I can't see us getting to the top today.'

'Not if those clouds unload, that's for sure. What time is it?'

'Four o'clock. Two hours' light left. Better get moving.'

I wasted valuable time trying to cross the rock band. It was tilted like a steep roof, but unlike the rock in the ramp it was black and compact with only a few small holds mostly hidden beneath the snow. I knew it wasn't difficult, but I was standing on an open face with a drop of nearly 4,000 feet below me and felt very unnerved by the exposure. There was also a long gap of unprotected rope between me and Simon who was belaying me from our resting place. His only anchor was his axes buried in the snow, and I knew all too well how useless these would be if I made a mistake.

My left foot slipped and the crampon points skittered on the rock. I hated this sort of delicate balance climbing, but I was committed to it now; no going back. As I balanced on two small edges of rock, front points teetering on the verge of slipping, my legs began to tremble and I shouted a warning to Simon. I could hear the fear in my voice and cursed myself for letting Simon know it. I tried moving up again, but my nerve failed me and I couldn't complete the move. I knew it would take just a couple of moves to reach easier ground, and tried convincing myself that if this wasn't so terrifyingly exposed I would walk up it, hands in pockets, but I couldn't shake off the fear. I was gripped.

Gradually, I calmed down and carefully thought out the few moves I needed to make. When I tried again I was surprised at how easy it seemed. I was above the difficulty and climbing quickly up easy ground before I realised it. The belay was little better than Simon's and I warned him of this before he started after me. The sudden fright still had me breathing hard and it annoyed me to see Simon climb easily over the difficulties and know that I had lost control and let fear get the better of me.

'God! I was gripped stupid on that,' I said.

'I noticed.'

'Which gully should we go for?' I had looked for a likely one but found it impossible to see, when close up to them, whether they closed off or not.

'I don't know. That one is the widest. I'll have a look at that.'

Simon entered the gully and immediately began floundering in deep powder. The sides of the flutings rose up fifteen feet on either side of him. There was no chance of changing line. Spindrift avalanches poured down on to his struggling figure so that sometimes he disappeared from sight. The light was going rapidly, and I noticed that it had begun to snow, the spindrift getting heavier. I was directly beneath Simon and, after sitting still for two hours, I was chilled to the bone. Simon was excavating huge quantities of snow down on to me and I could do nothing to avoid it.

I switched my head-torch on and was surprised to see that it was eight o'clock. Four hours to climb 300 feet. I seriously doubted whether we would be able to get up these flutings. At last, a distant, muffled shout from the snow-filled clouds told me to follow on. I was dangerously cold, despite having put on my polar jacket and windproof. We would have to bivouac somewhere on these horrendous slopes because sitting still for such a long time while belaying was out of the question. I couldn't believe what Simon had done to climb that rope length up the gully. He had dug a trench four feet deep by four wide all the way up it; his exhausting search for more solid snow yielding a weak layer of crusted ice which

47

barely held his weight. Most of this had been broken away as he had climbed, so that I had great difficulty following his lead. It had taken him three hours to climb, and when I reached him I could see that it had tired him out. I felt very tired, too, and cold, and it was important we bivouacked soon.

'I can't believe this snow!'

'Bloody terrifying. I thought I was falling off all the way up.'

'We have to bivi. I was freezing down there.'

'Yeah, but not here. The fluting has got too small.'

'Okay. You may as well lead up again.'

I knew it would be easier and avoid rope tangles, but I regretted not being able to keep moving. Two freezing and interminable hours later I joined Simon 100 feet higher up. He was belayed in a large hole he had dug into the base of the gully.

'I've found some ice.'

'Good enough for an ice screw?'

'Well it's better than nothing. If you get in here we can enlarge this sideways.'

I squeezed in beside him, fully expecting the floor of the cave to collapse down the gully at any moment. We began digging into the sides of the flutings, slowly enlarging the cave into a long rectangular snow hole set across the gully, with the entrance partially filled up by our excavations.

By eleven o'clock we had settled into our sleeping bags, eaten the last freeze-dried meal, and were savouring a last hot drink of the day.

'Three hundred feet to go. I just hope it isn't worse than what we've just done.'

'At least the storm has stopped. But it's damned cold. I think my little finger is frostbitten. It's white down to the hand.'

It must have been close to minus twenty when we had been exposed to the spindrift in the gullies, and the wind had brought the wind chill temperature down nearer to minus forty. We were lucky to have found a place for a snow-hole.

I hoped we would have clear sunny weather tomorrow.

The base of the gas canister was coated in a thick layer of ice. I knocked it against my helmet and managed to remove most of it, then I stuffed it deep into my sleeping bag, feeling the icy metal against my thighs. Five minutes later I was snuggled in again with only my nose sticking out of the bag, and one eye keeping a sleepy watch on the stove. It roared busily, but it was dangerously close to my bag. Blue light shone through the cave walls. It had been a long and bitterly cold night at 20,000 feet, perhaps nearer 21,000.

When the water was boiling I sat up and hurriedly donned my polar jacket, windproof and gloves. I fumbled in the snow wall of the cave looking for the sachet of fruit juice and the chocolate.

'Brew's ready.'

'God's teeth! I'm bloody freezing.'

Simon uncurled from his cramped foetal position, took the

steaming mug and disappeared back into his bag. I drank slowly, hugging the hot cup to my chest, watching the second lot of snow melt down in the pan. The gas flame was not so strong.

'How much gas have we got left?' I asked.

'One tin. Is that one empty?'

'Not quite. We may as well drink as much as it will produce and save the other for the descent.'

'Yeah. We haven't got much fruit juice left either. Just one packet.'

'We'll have judged it right, then. Enough for one more bivi, that's all we need.'

It was a long, cold business gearing up, but that was the least of my worries. The flutings lay ahead and it was my turn to lead. To make things more difficult I had to exit the cave and somehow climb over the roof, which stretched the full width of the gully. I succeeded, but not without destroying most of the cave and burying Simon, who had belayed me from inside. Once on to the slope of the gully I looked back down to where we had climbed the previous night. All traces of the trench dug by Simon had disappeared. It had been swept clean and refilled by the incessant waves of spindrift which had poured down the gully during the snowstorm. I was disappointed to see that the gully ended about 100 feet above me. The flutings on each side joined together to form a single razor-sharp ribbon of powder. I would have to try to cross over into another fluting after all.

The sky was clear and there was no wind. It was Simon's turn to sit stoically under the deluge of snow I was forced to kick down, but daylight had dubious advantages. It made the climbing easier and allowed me to see whether I was about to slip; on the other hand it provided unnerving glimpses between my legs of 4,500 feet of emptiness. Knowing that our belays were anything but secure and that any fall would be disastrous made me concentrate on the way ahead. As I approached the dead-end in the gully the angle steadily increased, and it became obvious that I would have to traverse out through the side fluting soon; but . . . which one? I couldn't see over the sides of the flutings and had no idea what I would be traversing into. I looked down and saw Simon watching me intently. Only his head and chest stuck out from the roof of the cave, and the huge drop framed behind him emphasised the precariousness of our position. I could see that the flutings were not as high near the cave, and that Simon might be able to see more of the way ahead than I could.

'Which way should I go? Can you see anything?'

'Don't go left.'

'Why?'

'It seems to drop away, and it looks bloody dangerous!'

'What's on the right?'

'Can't see, but the flutings are not so steep. It's a lot better than the left anyway.'

I hesitated. Once I started ploughing through a fluting I might be unable to return. I didn't want to find myself in an even worse position. However high I stretched I couldn't see into the gully on my right. I wasn't even sure there would be a gully there, and none of the snow I could see above me gave any idea of what might be awaiting me.

'Okay. Watch the ropes,' I shouted as I began to dig into the right-hand side of the gully. Then I laughed at what I had just said. It would do no good concentrating on belaying if the belay was going to rip straight out.

To my surprise, digging furiously with both axes into the fluting was no harder than climbing the gully, and I emerged, breathing hard, on the other side, in an identical steepening gully above which I could see the huge cornice of the summit only a rope's length away. Simon floundered up to me and whooped when he saw the summit behind me.

'Cracked it,' he said.

'I hope so, but this last bit looks bloody steep.'

'It'll go.' He set off up the slope churning huge amounts of freezing snow down on to my exposed belay hole. I pulled my hood over my helmet and turned my back, gazing down at the glacier far below me. Suddenly our exposed stance appalled me. The loose snow was so steep and my belay so precarious that I felt a sickening disbelief in what we were doing. An excited yell tore me from my thoughts and I turned to see the rope disappearing over the top of the gully above.

'Done it. No more flutings. Come up.'

He was sitting, legs astride a fluting, grinning manically, when I pulled myself wearily out of the gully. Behind him, less than fifty feet from us, the summit cornice reared up in a threatening bulge of snow-ice which overhung the West Face. I quickly moved past Simon and cramponed on firm snow up and to the left, where the summit cornice was smallest. Ten minutes later, I stood beneath the snow ridge dividing West Face from East.

'Take a photo.'

I waited until Simon had his camera ready before planting my axe over the ridge on to the east side and heaving myself over onto the broad-backed col under the summit. For the first time in four days I had a new view on which to feast. The sun bathed the snow sweeping down into the eastern glacier. After the long, cold, shadowed days on the West Face it felt luxurious to sit there warmed by the sun. I had forgotten that, now we were climbing in the Southern Hemisphere, everything was the wrong way round: South Faces here were the equivalent of icy cold North Faces in the Alps, and East Faces became West. No wonder the mornings had been so cold and shadowed and we had to wait until late in the day before being blessed with a few hours' sunshine.

Simon joined me and we laughed happily as we took off our sacks and sat on them, carelessly dropping axes and mitts in the snow, content to be quiet a while and look around us.

'Let's leave the sacks here and go up to the summit,' Simon said, interrupting my self-indulgent reverie. The summit! Of course, I had forgotten we had only reached the ridge. Escaping from the West Face had seemed to be an end in itself. I looked up at the icecream cone rising behind Simon. It was only about 100 feet away.

'You go ahead. I'll take some photos when you reach the top'.

He grabbed some chocolate and sweets before getting up

and tramping slowly up through soft snow. The altitude was having its effect. When he was outlined against the sky, bending over his axe on top of the spectacular summit cornice, I began feverishly snapping photographs. Leaving the sacks at the col, I followed, breathing hard, and feeling the tiredness in my legs.

We took the customary summit photos and ate some chocolate. I felt the usual anticlimax. What now? It was a vicious circle. If you succeed with one dream, you come back to square one and it's not long before you're conjuring up another, slightly harder, a bit more ambitious – a bit more dangerous. I didn't like the thought of where it might be leading me. As if, in some strange way, the very nature of the game was controlling me, taking me towards a logical but frightening conclusion; it always unsettled me, this moment of reaching the summit, this sudden stillness and quiet after the storm, which gave me time to wonder at what I was doing and sense a niggling doubt that perhaps I was inexorably losing control – was I here purely for pleasure or was it egotism? Did I really want to come back for more? But these moments were also good times, and I knew that the feelings would pass. Then I could excuse them as morbid pessimistic fears that had no sound basis.

'Looks like we are in for another storm,' Simon said.

He had been quietly examining the North Ridge, our line of descent, which was rapidly being obscured by massed clouds rolling up the East Face and tumbling out over on to the west side. Even now I could see little of the ridge, and the glacier up which we had made our approach would be completely covered within the hour. The ridge began where we had left our sacks and rose to a subsidiary summit before twisting back on itself and curling down into the clouds. I saw snatches of frighteningly steep razor-edges through cloud gaps, and some dangerously corniced sections, the East Face dropping away to the right in a continuous flank of tortured flutings. We would be unable to traverse below the corniced ridge at a safe distance. The flutings looked impassable.

'Jesus! It looks hairy.'

'Yeah. Better get our skates on. If we move quickly we can traverse under that summit and then rejoin the ridge further down. In fact, I don't think we'll even have an hour.'

Simon held out his hand, and the first snowflakes drifted down lazily on to his glove.

We returned to the sacks and then set off to circle around the minor summit. Simon led the way. We moved roped together, with coils of rope in hand in case of a fall. It was the fastest way and, with the deep powder snow hampering our progress, it was our only chance of getting past the minor summit in reasonable visibility. If Simon fell I hoped to have time enough to get my axe buried; though I doubted whether the axe would find any purchase in the loose snow.

The clouds closed in on us after half an hour, when we were on the east flank of the second summit. Ten minutes later we were lost in the white-out. There was no wind, and the snow fell silently in large heavy flakes. It was about two-thirty and we knew it would snow until late evening. We stood in silence, staring around us, trying to make out where we were.

'I think we should head down.'

'I don't know . . . no, not down. We must keep in touch with the ridge. Didn't you see those flutings on this side. We'd never get back up again.'

'Have we got past that second summit?'

'I think so, yes.'

'I can't see anything up there.'

The snow and cloud merged into a uniform blank whiteness. I could see no difference between snow and sky further than five feet from me.

'Wish we had a compass.'

As I spoke I noticed a lightening in the cloud above us. The sun, shining weakly through the murk, cast the faintest of shadows on the ridge 100 feet above us, but before I had a chance to tell Simon, it was gone.

'I've just seen the ridge.'

'Where?'

'Straight above us. Can't see a thing now, but I definitely saw it.'

'Right, I'll climb up and find it. If you stay here you'll have better luck stopping me if I don't see the edge of the ridge in time.'

He set off, and after a short time I had only the ropes moving through my hands to show me he was there. The snow fall was getting heavier. I felt the first twinges of anxiety. This ridge had turned out to be a lot more serious than we had ever imagined while our attention had been focused on the route up the West Face. I was about to call out to Simon and ask if he could see anything, but the words died on my lips as the ropes suddenly whipped out through my gloves. At the same time a deep, heavy explosion of sound echoed through the clouds. The ropes ran unchecked through my wet icy gloves for a few feet then tugged sharply at my harness, pulling me chest-first into the snow slope. The roaring died away.

I knew at once what had happened. Simon must have fallen through the corniced ridge, yet the volume of sound suggested something more like a serac avalanche. I waited. The ropes remained taut with his body weight.

'Simon!' I yelled. 'You okay?'

There was no answer. I decided to wait before attempting to move up towards the ridge. If he was hanging over the west side I reckoned it would be some time before he sorted himself out and managed to regain the ridge. After about fifteen minutes I heard Simon shouting unintelligibly. The weight had come off the rope, and I climbed towards him until I could make out what he was saying.

'I've found the ridge!'

I had gathered *that*, and laughed nervously. He had indeed found a lot more of the ridge than he had bargained for. I stopped grinning when I reached him. He was standing shakily just below the crest.

'I thought I'd had it there,' he muttered, suddenly sitting down heavily in the snow as if his legs had failed him. 'Bloody hell . . . that was it! The whole bloody thing fell off. God!'

He shook his head as if trying to dislodge what he had just seen. When the fright eased, and his body stopped pumping

55

adrenalin, he looked back at the edge of the ridge, and quietly told me what had happened:

'I never saw the ridge. I just glimpsed an edge of it far away to the left. There was no warning. No crack. One minute I was climbing, the next I was falling. It must have broken away forty feet back from the edge. It broke behind me, I think; or under my feet. Either way it took me down instantly. It was so *fast*! I had no time to think. I didn't know what the hell was going on, except that I was falling.'

'I'll bet!' I looked at the drop of the face behind him as he bowed his head and breathed hard, one hand on his thigh trying to stop the tell-tale tremor in his leg.

'I was tumbling all over the place and everything seemed to be happening in slow motion. I forgot I was tied to the rope. The noise and the falling – it just stopped me understanding anything. I can remember seeing all these huge blocks of snow falling with me, they fell at the same speed at first, and I thought "this is it". They were massive. Ten- . . . twenty-foot-square chunks.'

He was calmer now, but I shivered at the thought of what would have happened if I had moved up with him – it would have taken both of us.

'Then I felt the rope at my waist, but I thought it would just come down with me. I wasn't stopping, and all the blocks were smashing against me, flipping me over.'

He paused again, then continued: 'It was much lighter below me, and the blocks tumbled away from me down an enormous drop of space, spinning and breaking up. I kept getting glimpses of this as the snow walloped into me and spun me round . . . Perhaps I wasn't falling by then, but all the thumping and spinning made it feel as if I was. It seemed to be going on and on and on . . . I wasn't scared then, just totally confused and numb. As if real time was standing still and there was no longer time to be frightened.'

When he did finally stop, he was hanging in space, and could see over to his left the ridge still peeling away. The cloud on the east side blocked the view slightly, but great blocks of snow were falling from the cloud and went crashing down the face below, as if the ridge was breaking away from him.

'At first I was so disoriented I wasn't sure whether I was safe or not. I had to think it out before I realised that you had held my fall. The drop below me was horrific. I could see right down the West Face, 4,500 feet, clear all the way to the glacier. I was in a panic for a while. The huge drop had appeared so suddenly beneath me, and I was hanging thirty feet below the ridge line, not touching the slope. The headwall of the West Face was directly beneath me. I could see our route up the icefield!'

'If that cornice had come down we would just have disappeared without trace,' I ventured. 'How did you get back?'

'Well, I tried to get back on to the ridge, and it turned out to be one hell of a struggle. The break-line left by the cornice was vertical snow and nearly thirty feet high. I didn't know if what was left after the collapse was safe. When I finally got up I heard you shouting from down on the East Face and I was nearly too tired to answer. I still couldn't see an end to the fresh break-line on the ridge. It seemed close to 200 feet. Funny how the visibility cleared as soon as I fell. Five minutes later and I would have seen the danger.'

We were now faced with a very dangerous ridge which, although it had collapsed, was no safer as a result. We could see secondary fracture lines in the snow just back from the edge, and one particular fracture ran parallel to and only four feet away from the crest for as far as we could see.

4

On the Edge

There was no question of traversing lower down on the East Face for this was a continuous series of large flutings running down into the clouds which had closed over the void again several hundred feet below us. It had stopped snowing. The flutings would be impossibly slow and dangerous to climb across, and to descend lower would see us lost in the white-out conditions below the cloud. There were few choices left open to us. Simon stood up and began moving gingerly along the crest five feet from the edge, along the continual crack-line running away from us. I moved further down the East Face to wait until he had taken out all the slack rope. At least then I could stop him if the ridge broke away again, but eventually I would have to join him, and we would move together along the ridge.

As I climbed up to rejoin his tracks it occurred to me that I had felt a moment of anxiety only minutes before Simon had fallen. I had noticed this in the past and always wondered about it. There had been no good reason for the sudden stab of worry. We had been on the mountain for over fifty hours and perhaps had become attuned to potential threats; so much so that I had sensed something would happen without understanding quite what it would be. I didn't like this irrational theory, since anxiety had returned with a vengeance. I could see that Simon had also tensed up. The descent was already far more serious than we had reckoned.

I moved carefully. I watched the crack-line, checked I had put my feet exactly where Simon's footsteps were, and continued nervously 150 feet behind Simon, who had his back to me. I might have a chance if I saw him fall in time. I could throw myself down the opposite side of the ridge and expect the ropes to stop us as they sawed through the ridge. He would have little or no warning. He might hear me scream out, or hear the ridge break, but he would have to turn round to see which side I was falling down before he could jump to the safe side. It seemed to me that the most likely accident would involve the whole ridge collapsing, taking us both down in one very long breakaway of snow.

I saw the crack close up, and when I moved past it I breathed a sigh of relief. The ridge was slightly safer at last. Unfortunately it now dropped away steeply and twisted back on itself with each turn, huge cornices bulging out over the West Face. I saw that these difficulties eased further in the distance so I wasn't surprised when Simon began descending the East Face. He intended to lose enough height to be able to traverse directly across to the easier section and avoid descending the tortured ridge. The easier ground lay a couple of hundred feet below our point on the ridge. I guessed how far we needed to descend before following Simon down.

We hadn't descended far before I realised how poor the light had become. I checked my watch and was surprised to see that it had gone five o'clock. We had left the summit nearly three and a half hours earlier and yet had made little progress along the ridge. It would be dark in an hour and, to make things more difficult, the storm clouds had boiled over us again and snowflakes were blowing up from the east into our faces. The temperature had also dropped sharply and, with the wind building up, it felt icy cold whenever we stopped.

Simon descended a gully between two flutings. I followed slowly, trying to keep the distance between us by moving only when the ropes moved. I descended into a uniform whiteness, snow and cloud merging into one. After a while I decided that we must have reached a point where we could now traverse horizontally across to the easier ground, but Simon carried on down. I shouted for him to stop, but received only a muffled reply. I yelled louder and the ropes stopped moving through my gloves. Neither of us could understand the other's shouts, so I moved down to get within earshot. I was alarmed to find that the gully became steeper and I kept slipping. I turned round to face into the slope, but it was still hard to remain in control.

I was close to him when I heard Simon shout again and could hear his query about why we had stopped. At that moment the snow whooshed away from under my feet and I dropped swiftly. I had both axes dug deep into the gully but they didn't stop me. I screamed a warning, and suddenly bumped heavily against Simon, stopping jammed up against him.

'Jesus! . . . I . . . Oh shit! I thought we'd had it . . . this is fucking stupid!'

Simon said nothing. I leant face first into the gully and tried to calm down. My heart seemed to be trying to hammer its way out of my chest, and my legs shook weakly. It had been fortunate that I was so close to Simon when I fell, not too far above to have built up enough speed to knock him down.

'You okay?' Simon asked.

'Yes. Scared . . . that's all.'

'Yeah.'

'We've gone far too low.'

'Oh! I was thinking perhaps we could descend all the way into the eastern glacier bay.'

'You're joking! Bloody hell! I've just nearly killed both of us on this bit, and we haven't a clue what it's like below us.'

'But that ridge is crazy. We'll never get down it tonight.'

'We're not getting off this tonight, anyway. For God's sake, it's almost dark now. If we rush off down there we'll be lucky if we ever get off this bloody thing.'

'Okay . . . okay, calm down. It was just an idea.'

'Sorry. I was freaked out. Couldn't we traverse out sideways from here and get back to the ridge where it drops down?'

'Okay. . . you first.'

I sorted out the tangles from my fall and then began digging into the right side of the fluting. An hour and a half later I had managed to cross innumerable flutings and gullies, and Simon was following a rope's-length behind me. We had covered less than 200 feet, and by then it was snowing hard, bitterly cold and windy. It was also dark and we were having to use our head-torches.

Stumbling through a wall of sugary snow and into another gully, I kicked against rock beneath the snow.

'Simon!' I shouted. 'Stop where you are a while. There's a small rock wall here. It's a bit tricky getting round it.'

I decided to place a rock peg in the wall, and then tentatively balance round the obstacle. I succeeded with the rock peg but somehow managed to fall down and round the wall without coming on to the rope. Simon employed an equally basic climbing technique using gravity and body weight, jumping down the wall without being able to see where he would land, but correct in the assumption that, when he did, it would be with such force that he would safely bury himself firmly in the loose snow beyond. The only flaw I could find in his reasoning was that he didn't know whether his landing would be loose snow or rock! We were too tired and cold by then to care.

Once beyond the rock we crossed an open slope of powder, mercifully without flutings. We were heading back up towards where we guessed the ridge would be, and after a couple of rope-lengths found a large cone of snow swept up against a rock wall. We decided to dig a snow cave.

Simon's head-torch kept flickering from a loose or damaged connection. I began digging and soon struck rock. I tried digging parallel with the rock, to make a long narrow cave, but after half an hour gave up. The cave had so many holes in it that it would provide little protection from the wind. It was bitterly cold, and Simon had struggled to repair his head-torch with his bare fingers, fiddling with the copper contacts in the dark. Digging had kept me warm, despite the temperature falling to around the minus twenty mark, but two of Simon's fingers were frostbitten. He became angry with me when I started to dig another cave. Unjustly, I

decided that Simon was behaving petulantly and ignored him.
The next site for the cave was marginally better and although
I struck rock I managed to build it to fit the two of us. By then
Simon had mended the torch but his fingers were beyond
rewarming. He was still bristling with anger at my lack of co-
operation.

I prepared the meal. There was little enough left. We ate
chocolate and dried fruit and drank a lot of fruit juice. By then
we had forgotten our tired anger and regained a sense of
perspective. I had been as cold and tired as Simon, and had
only wanted a cave dug quickly so that we could get into our
sleeping bags and make some hot drinks. It had been another
very long day. It had started well, and we had been glad to get
off the West Face, but the descent had become increasingly
difficult and nerve-wracking. Falling over the cornice had
shaken both of us, and the strain afterwards had been
wearing. We had got angry enough with each other today,
and more of the same wouldn't help.

Simon showed me his fingers, which had slowly come back
to life. But the index finger on each hand remained white and
solid as far back as the first knuckle. So, he had frostbite. I
hoped it would not suffer further damage the next day.
However, I felt sure that we were close to the end of the
difficulties on the ridge, and that we would be able to reach
base camp by the following afternoon. We only had enough
gas left for two drinks in the morning, but that should be
enough. As I settled myself down for sleep I couldn't shake off
the dread feelings I had experienced while traversing the
ridge. The image of the two of us falling helplessly down the
East Face, still roped together, had all too nearly come true. I
shuddered at the prospect of such an end. I knew Simon must
have felt the same. The year before he had witnessed just such
a terrible accident at the Croz Spur, high in the Mont Blanc
range of the French Alps. Two Japanese climbers had fallen to
their deaths from close to where he stood, only a short
distance from the top of the route.

For three days stormy weather had produced atrocious
conditions. The rocks were plastered in verglas, a hard patina

of ice covering the holds and filling the cracks. Progress had been painfully slow as each hold was chipped clear, and otherwise easy sections had become desperately extreme climbing. Simon and his partner, Jon Sylvester, had bivouacked twice on the face, and late in the afternoon of that third day, another storm was building up – the temperature plummeting, heavy clouds shrouding them in a world of their own, and the first spindrift powder snow avalanches sweeping down.

The two Japanese climbers had been following them closely. They had bivouacked separately, and there was no communication between the two teams, nor was there any sense of competitiveness or a suggestion that they might join forces. Both parties were coping equally well in the difficult conditions. There were frequent falls, often from the same points. They had watched one another struggle, fall, and try again as they progressed up the face.

When they reached the summit headwall Simon had seen the leading Japanese climber fall outwards and backwards, arms outstretched in surprise. The awesome 2,500-foot plunge, visible through breaks in the cloud, was framed behind him. To his horror, he had then seen the falling leader jerk and twist and, without a sound, pull his partner into the void. Their belay piton had torn free. The two men plunged down, roped together, helpless.

Simon had struggled up to Jon's stance, which was out of sight of that lower section, and told him what had happened. They stood quietly on the small rock ledge in the gathering storm trying to absorb the enormity of what had just taken place so close to them. There was nothing they could do for the two men, who would never have survived the fall, and the quickest way to get news to the rescue services would be over the summit and down into Italy.

As they resumed the climb they were shocked to hear a ghastly screaming from far below – the chilling sounds of someone in agony, desperately alone and terrified. Looking down, they saw the two climbers sliding down the upper icefield at ever-increasing speed 600 feet below them. They were still roped together, and various scattered items of gear and their rucksacks tumbled alongside them. All Simon could do was to stare helplessly at the two tiny figures racing down the ice. Then they were gone: disappearing over the lip of the icefield, falling out of view into the horrendous drop to the glacier.

By some desperate quirk at least one of the climbers must have survived the initial fall on to the icefield. Somehow they had been stopped, probably with their rope snagged on some rocky projection – but they weren't saved. It was a cruel twist, both for the victims and for the horrified spectators far above them. Only a short reprieve, five minutes or so, while one of them fought to make himself safe and find some anchor. Badly injured, he had had little chance. Perhaps he had slipped, or the rope had unsnagged: whatever had happened, the outcome was brutally final.

Simon and Jon, their confidence shattered, minds numbed by it all, had turned and struggled on up to the summit. It had been so sudden. They hadn't conversed with the two Japanese, but a mutual understanding and respect had developed. If they had all got down safely, then they would have talked, shared food on the long walk to the valley, met up in a bar in town, perhaps become friends.

I could remember seeing Simon walking slowly into the camp-site outside Chamonix when he got back. He was subdued and looked drawn and tired. He had sat numb, repeatedly questioning why his own tumble had been held on the same piton just before the Japanese leader had fallen and ripped it out. A day later he was his normal self again: an experience absorbed, shelved in his memory, understood and accepted, and left at that.

As sleep crept swiftly through me I tried to shake off the thought of how close we had come to the same appalling end as those two Japanese. There would have been no one to watch us, I thought: as if it would have made any difference.

I had the stove burning away cheerfully by my side, and could look beyond it through a hole in the snow cave. The East Face